ROCKS & MINERALS

A PORTRAIT OF THE NATURAL WORLD

Frederick D. Atwood

TODTRI

This book is dedicated with thanksgiving to my parents,
who have always supported and nurtured my love for nature,
to Miss Miriam Dickey, my "bird club" teacher
who taught me how to find all sorts of exciting things everywhere I looked,
and to the Creator, who made rocks and minerals
and gave us the ability to appreciate them.

This book was designed and produced by Todtri Productions Limited
P.O. Box 572, New York, NY 10116-0572   Fax (212) 695-6984
e-mail : info@todtri.com
Printed and bound in Korea

Library of Congress Catalog Card Number 97-066038
ISBN 1-57717-027-X
Visit us on the web!
www.todtri.com
Author: Frederick D. Atwood

Publisher: Robert M. Tod
Editorial Director: Elizabeth Loonan
Senior Editor: Cynthia Sternau
Project Editor: Ann Kirby
Photo Editor: Edward Douglas
Picture Researchers: Laura Wyss, Meiers Tambeau
Production Coordinator: Jay Weiser
Designer: Mark Weinberg
Typesetting: Command-O, NYC

PHOTO CREDITS

Photographer/Page Number

Frederick D. Atwood 3, 4, 5, 8–9, 13, 17, 27 (bottom), 29, 30, 31 (top), 32, 38 (top), 42, 44 (top and bottom), 46 (top and bottom), 47 (top and bottom), 50, 51 (bottom), 58, 59, 60 (bottom), 61, 62, 63, 64 (bottom), 65, 67, 68 (bottom), 70

E. R. Degginger 7 (top and bottom), 11 (top and bottom), 12 (top and bottom), 14 (top and bottom), 15, 16 (top and bottom), 18, 19 (top and bottom), 20 (top and bottom), 21, 22 (top and bottom), 23 (top and bottom), 24–25, 26, 27 (top), 28 (top and bottom), 31 (bottom), 33, 34 (top and bottom), 35 (top and bottom), 36, 37 (top and bottom), 38 (bottom), 39, 43 (bottom), 45, 49 (bottom), 51 (top and center), 64 (top), 66 (top and bottom)

Dembinsky Photo Associates
Willard Clay 53
Adam Jones 55
Rod Planck 6, 49 (top)

Picture Perfect
Graeme Gillies 69
Bill Holden 40–41
Joe McDonald 56–57
Scott T. Smith 10, 48, 52 (top), 68 (top)

Tom Stack & Associates
John Cancalosi 60 (top)
David M. Dennis (52 (bottom)
Doug Sokell (71)
Spencer Swanger (54)
Greg Vaughn 43 (top)

INTRODUCTION

This lava bridge in the Galapagos Islands formed where molten lava hit the cold ocean; erosion from wave-action probably played a role in its shape.

When I was eight I was excited by rocks. I could find them everywhere: in my back yard, on the beach, at the edge of a freshwater pond, by the side of the road on my way to school. As I walked, my pockets bulged with new treasures. Each new rock added to my collection was like a gem to me: schist decorated by sparkling flecks of mica; "lucky stones"—wave-worn pebbles completely encircled by a ring of quartz; gneiss with its swirling, banded patterns like fudge ripple ice cream; smooth, wave-polished, brightly colored granite (especially colorful when licked); rocks that looked like chunks of chocolate; rocks I could bend and see through; rocks that tasted salty and could melt the ice on my front steps; smooth, flat, layered rocks that I could skip across the pond; rocks that sparked and smelled like a match when I hit them together; rocks that could scratch glass; and rocks that I could crumble to bits with my bare hands.

Everywhere I went I saw how we used rocks: the salt-and-pepper-colored granite curbstones that edged my street, the white marble gravel in the driveway of my grandmother's neighbor, the smoothly polished, swirling green serpentine marble counter at the bank, the sparkling diamonds and shining gold in my grandmother's ring, and the carved alabaster cameo brooch she wore to church. When I looked closely at the concrete sidewalk, I saw that it was made out of sand: finely ground rocks. My grandfather even fed rocks (grit) to his parakeet to help it digest its birdseed. The chalkboard at school was slate, and even the chalk my teacher used to write with was a rock. It was made out of the

calcium-rich skeletons of microscopic life deposited in the oceans over millions of years. I wrote with rocks, too—the "lead" of my pencil was a rock called graphite. It was made out of pure carbon just as diamond was, but how different the two rocks were! "What an amazing world we live in," I thought, "and what amazing things rocks are. Where did they come from?" I wondered, "and how were they formed?"

Before too many years had passed, however, my interest in birds, insects, and plants surpassed my fascination with rocks. My attention shifted from the ground to the tree-tops. My collection of natural treasures expanded to include feathers, seeds, and butterflies. My reading focused on bird behavior and edible plants. By high school, a rock was just a rock. But since then I have canoed in the Chihuahuan Desert, awed by the spectacular canyons that were carved by the Rio Grande through the fossil-rich sedimentary rock deposited in an extinct ancient sea. I have hiked on the rumbling flanks of active volcanoes with my eyes watering and my nose running from the sulfurous "rotten egg" fumes. And I have stood on an arrete, a

narrow wall of rock carved by back-to-back valley glaciers, along the Continental Divide, exulting in the glacier-polished rocks and the glorious U-shaped valley carved by the glacier below me.

From these experiences I have gained a new appreciation of the majesty and beauty of rocks and minerals and their significance in determining the shape of the land and the nature of the soil and the ecosystems that live upon it. The massive forces and intense temperatures that form rocks and minerals in the depths of the earth and violently—or patiently—shove them up into towering mountains is mind-boggling. The eons it takes for rain, ice, and wind to whittle away a mountain, carrying it grain by grain into the sea, or for a river to scrape, grind, swirl, and dissolve its way down through a thousand feet of sedimentary rock, forming a towering canyon, is almost incomprehensible. I am amazed when I pick up a piece of sandstone and realize that the extinct snails preserved in it once lived in an ocean that ebbed and flowed fifty million years ago where now it is dry land, thousands of feet up a mountain, hundreds of miles from the sea. It is humbling to think that the sand in this rock has been recycled for billions of years, from magma to quartz crystals in granite or a quartz vein in the bedrock at the roots of a mountain, to sand, to sandstone, to sand, to metamorphic quartzite . . . eventually recycled back to magma as one section of the earth's crust slid beneath another, to resurface again somewhere else and continue the cycle—the same atoms in different forms in different places for the 4.5 billion years of the earth's history When we are gone, this rock will ultimately find its way back home to the warm, cozy sea of magma. Perhaps next time some of its atoms will come back to the surface in a violent volcanic eruption and float across the ocean as a piece of pumice.

The Rio Grande River carved Santa Elena Canyon in Big Bend National Park, Texas. Over a thousand feet of limestone tower above these canoers as they maneuver around fallen boulders and try to comprehend the mind-boggling amount of time it took to form this awe-inspiring landscape.

THE SIGNIFICANCE OF ROCKS AND MINERALS

Practically everything we do or use in our daily lives depends on materials extracted from the ground. The history of man's exploration of the world and our waging of war has often centered around obtaining access to strategic mineral resources that are usually the basis for the wealth of a nation. The lust for gold funded much of the exploration and conquest of the Americas by Europeans. Some modern-day conflicts, such as the Persian Gulf War and conflicts between indigenous people and oil companies in the Amazon Basin, are rooted in our dependence on oil or other mineral resources.

Uses of Rocks and Minerals

Look around you now and see all the things that are made out of rocks and minerals mined from the ground. The paper of this book, though mostly plant fiber, has probably been synthesized using kaolin, sulfur, and barium (from barite). The film used to photograph the illustrations uses silver mined from the ores argentite and chlorargyrite. Metals, extracted from ores such as hematite (iron),

sphalerite (zinc), bauxite (aluminum), cuprite (copper), galena (lead), nickeline (nickel), and cassiterite (tin), have given us all kinds of metal objects including cans, cars, coins, building materials, and alloys such as pewter, bronze, brass, and stainless steel. The ubiquitous material plastic, which we use more of than steel, aluminum, and copper combined, is synthesized from petroleum, the mineral remains of ancient plankton. Petroleum is also used to make the rayon, Dacron polyester, or nylon you may be wearing, the gasoline that powers your automobile, and over

Quartz occurs in many forms and colors, but clear crystals like this are rare. Clear quartz is used in making lenses and is an important component of watches, television, and radar apparatus. Striking two pieces of quartz together will produce a spark and a match-like odor.

Pebble beaches are excellent places to search for stones that have been beautifully rounded and polished by the churning surf. This beach has quartz, porphyry, basalt, and gneiss mixed with an abundance of granite.

Some minerals occur in flower-like formations like these barite roses. Barium, extracted from barite, shows up well in x-rays and is used medically to help diagnose disorders of the digestive tract. This Rumanian specimen also contains realgar, an ore of the toxic element arsenic.

Following page: Where rocks grind past each other along fault lines, they fragment into angular chunks of rock of varying sizes. These may then be surrounded by a mineral matrix and resolidify like this breccia specimen from Texas.

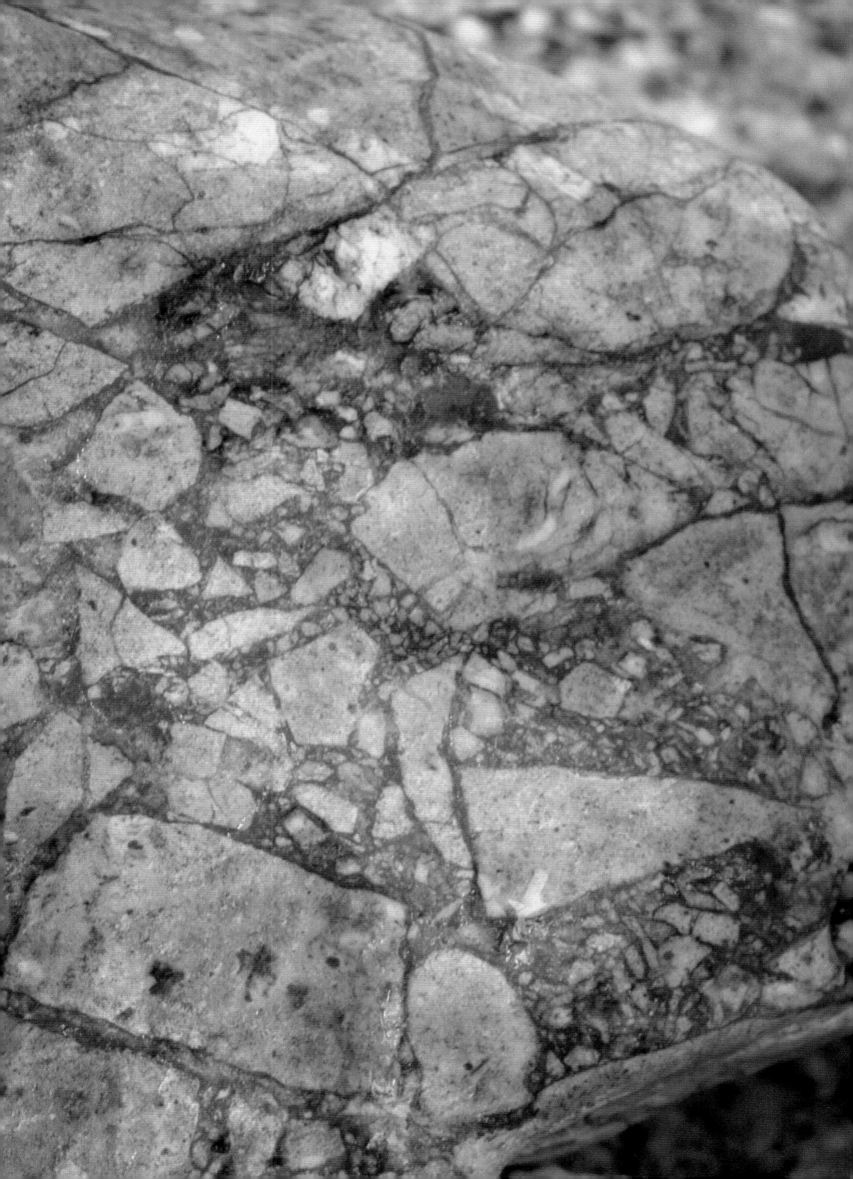

175 different compounds used by the chemical industry to make everything from cosmetics to toothpaste to carpets. Electricity, carried by aluminum power lines and copper wires to the glowing tungsten filaments (from wolframite) of your incandescent light bulbs, may have been generated using fossil fuels (coal or petroleum) or nuclear power, which depends on uranium ores such as uraninite, pitchblende, and carnotite. The fertilizers used to grow your fruits and vegetables may contain pulverized gypsum or limestone to reduce acidity, and apatite or sylvite to add phosphate. The insecticides and herbicides used to kill pests on these crops may have been made using coal extracts, arsenic, barium, sulfur, or fluoride. Quartz, mica, silver, copper and gallium may be critical components of your computer, television, watch or other electronic equipment.

Look out your window. The window itself is made from soda ash, limestone, and melted quartz sand, which is high in silica content. The cars driving by may have shiny, non-rusting chrome trim, extracted from chromium ore (chromite); platinum, rhodium, or palladium to remove air pollution in their catalytic converters; tin, a tough, corrosion-resistant metal often used in bearings; and cobalt, zinc, or titanium in their paint. The road the cars are driving on is made out

Sphalerite is an ore of zinc, and is useful in making brass, galvanized steel, and batteries. Since sphalerite also contains sulfur, it smells like rotten eggs if hydrochloric acid is added to it. Sphalerite emits flashes of light when it is scratched in a dark room.

of asphalt (dolomite and other rocks mixed with the tar-like bitumen resulting from coal or petroleum processing) and is probably laid down on a bed of gravel of crushed igneous rocks like basalt, gabbro, and diabase, which are noted for their toughness. The airplane passing overhead may contain titanium (from rutile), which is lightweight and highly resistant to high temperatures; an alloy of nickel and niobium (from columbite), which is strong and corrosion resistant and can withstand the high temperatures generated by a jet engine; and magnesium (from dolomite and magnesite), which is even lighter than aluminum. Other metallic minerals added to change the properties of steel

These limestone outcrops in Utah are being eroded by weather and by acids secreted by the lichens growing on their surface. As rocks are eroded they determine the characteristics of the soils around them. Limestone generally neutralizes soil acidity, thus affecting which plants can live there.

Graphite, like diamond, is pure carbon; but diamond is the hardest mineral, while graphite is one of the softest. Graphite's softness makes it useful in pencil lead, and its slippery feel makes it a good lubricant for machinery.

Occasionally gypsum's tabular crystals form in a rose-like cluster called a desert rose. Gypsum also occurs in huge deposits up to ten meters thick which precipitated out of seawater as ancient seas evaporated. Gypsum is an important ingredient of paint, cement, and plaster.

frequently dislocated shoulder. Medicines may incorporate sulfur or mercury or compounds extracted from dolomite (Milk of Magnesia), epsomite (Epsom salts), bismuthite (Pepto-Bismol) or coal. The lead apron used to protect your gonads from mutagenic x-rays probably came from the ore galena. The x-rays were generated using tungsten (from wolframite) or thulium (from fluorite). Platinum, radium, and cobalt are used in chemotherapy for cancer. Barium shows up well in x-rays so it is often injected into the digestive system to help doctors visualize and diagnose medical problems such as cancer or bowel disorders.

Granite, sandstone, limestone, marble, and gneiss are the most frequently used building stones. Granites are relatively resistant to weathering, and their low iron content keeps them from becoming stained with rust. Many building stones are polished for decorative use in floors, tiles, foundations, walls, and counters. Limestone and marble building blocks often contain such spectacular fossils that some museums and universities conduct field trips along city streets to study the geology and paleontology revealed in the building stones!

The brownstone buildings common in many of America's eastern cities are made out of 230 million-year-old Triassic sandstones, which are easily carved. The iron

alloys include vanadium, manganese, molybdenum, and tungsten.

Have you recently had medical attention? The surgeon's cutting instruments may have been made from the metal tantalum (from tantalite ore). Perhaps an orthopedic surgeon fastened your bones together using a titanium screw like the one used to repair my

For as long as humans have existed, we have used rocks that break with a hard, sharp cutting-edge to make stone tools. This volcanic rhyolite was fashioned into a hand ax over a million years ago. Obsidian, quartz, flint, and chert were the most commonly used minerals by prehistoric tool-makers.

oxide which cements the sand grains together in this sandstone gives it a brownish color and makes it more durable and weather resistant. The Egyptian pyramids are made out of limestone. Cement, concrete, and bricks are made out of rocks like marble, quartz, dolomite, shale, and limestone. Gypsum is used to make plaster, plasterboard, and tiles. Flagstones and roofing tiles are often made out of slate. Vinyl siding for houses is made weather-resistant by the incorporation of tin.

The Influence of
Rocks and Minerals on Local Ecology

As rocks are thrust to the surface by geological forces, and as they are weathered by local climate, they determine the shape of the land, the flow of weather systems, soil types, and therefore, local ecosystems. Some rare ecological communities, for instance, are specialized to grow only on soils formed from decomposing serpentine, which is rich in magnesium but poor in calcium.

As rocks decompose by chemical weathering to form soil, the texture of the soil is determined by the crystal size of the parent rock. Granite and rhyolite are made out of the same minerals, but rhyolite is formed by magma, which cools more quickly, forming smaller crystals than in granite. Therefore, rhyolite forms a more finely textured soil than granite. The same holds true for the comparison of fine-grained basalt to coarser-grained gabbro. This basic difference in the parent rocks affects the ecology of the communities living in the soils formed from them. Generally, finely textured soils are less permeable to water, contain more nutrients and less oxygen, and remain wet longer than coarse-grained soils. All of this determines what kinds of plants grow best in those soils.

The type of rock also affects the acidity or alkalinity of the soil that forms from it. For

Galena is easily identified by its silvery, metallic luster, its chunky, step-like cleavage, and its hefty feel. It is an ore of lead that has been smelted for centuries; some historians believe that poisoning from lead water pipes may have contributed to the fall of the Roman Empire.

Orpiment is an arsenic ore which generally forms in low temperature veins or as a crust around hot springs. Most arsenic-bearing minerals smell like garlic when heated.

Mica is one of the most common minerals, usually occurring as small silvery sparkles in rocks like granite, gneiss, and schist. This Brazilian specimen of muscovite shows that mica also occurs in large stacks of sheet-like layers that resemble the pages of a book.

instance, limestone forms alkaline soils with a pH greater than seven. The pH of the soil affects the availability of nutrients to the plants growing in the soil. Acid soil (low pH) is generally poorer in nitrogen, phosphate, copper, calcium, magnesium, and potassium than more alkaline soils. Alkaline and neutral soils are generally poorer in iron and manganese than more acidic soils. All of these nutrients are important to plants, but different plants are specialized to live in soils with differing nutrient levels. Often one can accurately predict the presence or absence of limestone in the bedrock underlying a region by looking at the types of plants growing in the area. Maidenhair fern*(Adiantum)*, sycamore *(Plantanus)*, possum haw *(Ilex decidua)*, and black walnut *(Juglans)* typically grow in neutral to alkaline soils, while pink lady slipper *(Cypripedium acaule)*, chainfern *(Woodwardia)*, blueberry *(Vaccinium)*, trailing arbutus *(Arbutus unedo)*, and sphagnum moss *(Sphagnum)* are known for their ability to thrive in more acidic soils. Soil pH is also significant for agriculture. Since most crops grow best in a neutral pH range, farmers may have to add lime (from limestone) or other minerals to adjust the soil pH.

The type of rock from which a soil is formed also affects what nutrients are present. Phosphorus comes from apatite and other phosphate rocks. Potassium comes from decomposing feldspar, mica, and clay. Magnesium weathers out of hornblende, serpentine, olivine, and biotite. Important calcium-releasing minerals are calcite, apatite, dolomite, gypsum, and calcium feldspars. Most boron, required by plants for sugar metabolism, comes from the beautiful mineral tourmaline.

Just as geology affects the health of plants by determining what nutrients are present, it also affects the health of the animals that graze on those plants. Animals require cobalt to make vitamin B_{12}, which is needed to make red blood cells properly. The early settlers of New England noticed that in certain areas of New Hampshire and Cape Cod, the cattle were suffering from a mysterious disease known locally as "Chocorua's Curse" or "Neck's Ail." Apparently the soils on which these cattle grazed were derived from deposits that had been scraped from the

cobalt-poor granites of the White Mountains by glaciers and deposited when the glaciers melted. As a result, thousands of years later, the grass the cattle ate had no cobalt, and the cattle became anemic. It is also possible for grass to be toxic to cattle if, for instance, it is growing in soil that has excessive amounts of a nutrient such as molybdenum. The cattle in certain moist valleys of Nevada and California where the surrounding granite mountains have a very high molybdenum content suffer from molybdenum toxicity. Some historians even relate the demise of General George Custer at Little Big Horn in Montana to a similar problem. It seems that Custer's horses may have performed poorly in battle because they suffered from selenium poisoning, which resulted from their overwintering in an area rich in selenium rocks. Sitting Bull's horses came from a different area where the selenium levels were lower. His healthy horses performed well.

The type of exposed or underlying rock and the resulting soil present is also important for civil engineers as they design highways, drainage systems, and large buildings. Even insurance companies and money-lending organizations make use of this information as they determine insurance rates or security for loans.

Sulfur is one of the most widely used minerals in the chemical industry. Since it has a low melting point, it often occurs in deposits around geothermal vents and hot springs. It is mined by pumping super-heated water into deposits, melting it out.

Millerite is a nickel ore that frequently occurs as a mass of radiating hair-like crystals. Nickel is a metal used to make magnets, coins, electrical heating wire, and corrosion-resistant steel.

Fluorite forms perfect cubic crystals which are sometimes green or violet. It is a source of fluoride which is added to toothpaste to prevent tooth decay. Yttrium—a rare element used to make superconductors, lasers, and television screens—can also be extracted from fluorite.

Snail fossils in sandstone high in the mountains and far from the sea are evidence of the constantly changing conditions on earth.

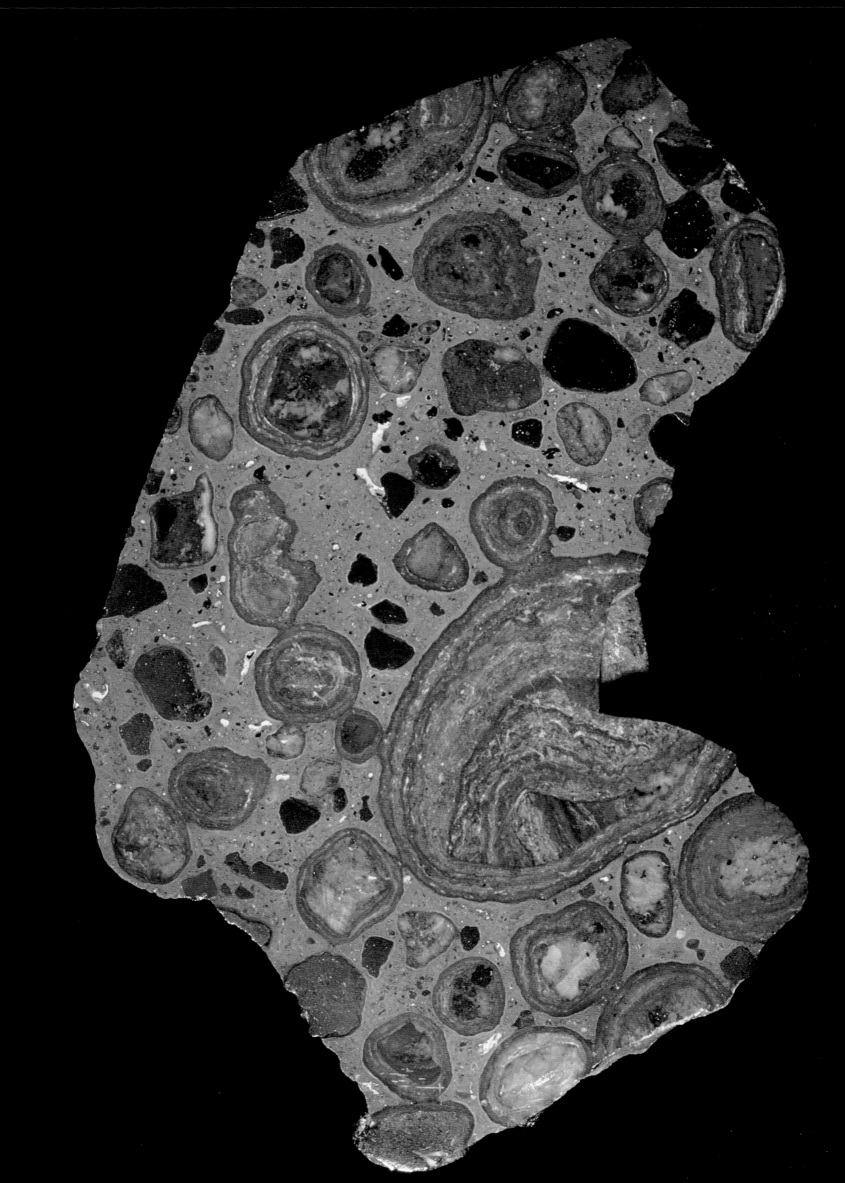

MINERALS

What is a Mineral?

The basic atoms out of which all matter is constructed are called elements. These elements are organized in specific ways, based on their electron configurations, to form the basic minerals that are the building blocks of all inorganic matter. There are nearly three thousand known minerals, but most of these are harder to find than gold. Only about one hundred minerals are very common. Minerals are classified by their atomic make-up as well as by their specific physical and chemical properties. Such properties include the shape and growth pattern of the crystals they form; other non-crystalline shapes in which they occur (branching, crust-like, or shaped like a bunch of grapes, a flower, or a kidney); their response to acid, water, and heat; the cleavage, or fracture pattern, they exhibit when they are chipped; their ability to conduct electricity; the color of their "streak" when scraped on a piece of unglazed porcelain; the way they reflect light (their luster); their color (though this can be quite variable for many minerals); their density (specific gravity); and their "hardness."

The hardness of a mineral is determined by what other minerals or objects they can scratch or be scratched by. Talc, a very soft rock with a hardness rating of one, can be scratched by a fingernail or any other mineral with hardness greater than one. Since it is so soft, talc, also known as soapstone, has been carved into figurines, artwork, and kitchenware since prehistoric times. Calcite, with a hardness of three, cannot be scratched by a fingernail, but can be scratched by a penny. Beautiful green or purple crystals of fluorite, with a hardness of four, can scratch a penny and calcite, but can themselves be scratched by an iron nail. Because of this fragility, fluorite is generally not very useful

Corundum is the second hardest mineral; only diamond is harder. Ruby is the red form of corundum, colored by tiny amounts of the element chromium. This uncut specimen is from Burma.

as a gem. Glass, with a hardness of five, can scratch apatite, a rock with the same chemical composition as your bones and teeth. But orthoclase feldspar, one of the most common minerals found in granite, with a hardness of six, can scratch glass. So can quartz, the main ingredient of sand. Quartz has a hardness of seven and can be scratched by a steel file, but not by the knife blade that can scratch orthoclase. The dazzling gem topaz, with a hardness of eight, can even scratch a steel file, but it can be scratched by sandpaper made from the common mineral corundum, whose hardness is nine. The ruby, emerald, and sapphire are rare gem forms of corundum. Notice that the most valuable gems are among the strongest minerals. The hardest

Labradorite is a colorful form of feldspar that is often used as a gem. It can be blue or green, and sometimes has inclusions which reflect the light in a scintillating display of color called schillerization.

This marvelous specimen of sedimentary rock from South Africa is a cross-section of nearly-spherical hematite concretions which accumulated in layers around pebbles. Hematite is an iron ore, which when ground to a powder, is blood-red. Its name is derived from the Greek word for blood.

This zinc ore composed of cleiophane, sphalerite, and willemite looks like just an ordinary rock when viewed under normal white light. . .

. . . but when viewed under ultraviolet light these minerals fluoresce with unexpected brilliance, converting the invisible ultraviolet light into dazzling colors of visible light.

mineral of all is the diamond; with its sparkling beauty and a hardness of ten, it lives up to its Greek name, which means "invincible."

Some Unique Properties of Minerals

Minerals have an amazing variety of other interesting properties, some of which are quite peculiar. Uranium ores are radioactive. Magnetite, an iron ore, is magnetic, while franklinite, siderite, and hematite become magnetic when heated. Some minerals change color when heated: yellow topaz turns pink; zircon changes from brown to blue; greenish blue aquamarine (beryl) turns a deeper blue.

Some minerals do wonderful things with light. Fluorite, cerussite, and several ores of zinc and uranium are fluorescent, glowing in psychedelic shades of green, orange, and violet when ultraviolet light is shined on them. During World War II the fluorescence of scheelite helped amateurs and professionals locate this very important ore of tungsten, a metal that was greatly needed for the war effort. Other minerals, such as willemite, a zinc ore, are phosphorescent, emitting an eerie green glow for several minutes after the light is turned out. Phosphorescent minerals are used to make the glow-in-the-dark paint on watches. Quartz, flint, sphalerite, and pyrite all produce flashes of light when struck by various hard objects. Bornite, an iron ore, is also known as "peacock ore" because it dazzles the eyes with its blue, red, and purple iridescence. Three forms of feldspar—albite, moonstone, and labradorite—are sometimes considered gemstones when they have small rod-like inclusions of other minerals, such as iron oxide, that reflect a glistening array of colors (schillerization). Small crystals of rutile in some specimens of rose quartz and star sapphire cause the light entering the crystal to be "asteriated"—refracted back out in a star-like pattern. Such specimens are highly treasured gems. Cryolite, a colorless crystal sometimes found in pegmatite veins, seems to magically disappear when it is placed in water because it

Willemite and calcite fluoresce under ultraviolet light. Fluorescence is a characteristic of very few minerals. Willemite is also phosphorescent; it glows in the dark after a normal light is turned off.

Chalcopyrite is an ore of both copper and iron; it often contains silver and gold as well. This tarnished specimen from South Africa displays a rainbow of colorful iridescence. It is often found with bornite, known as peacock ore because of its similar iridescence.

Jasper is also a type of chalcedony. Its rich chestnut-red color and intricate patterns make it a treasured ornamental stone. This formation from California is called orbicular jasper.

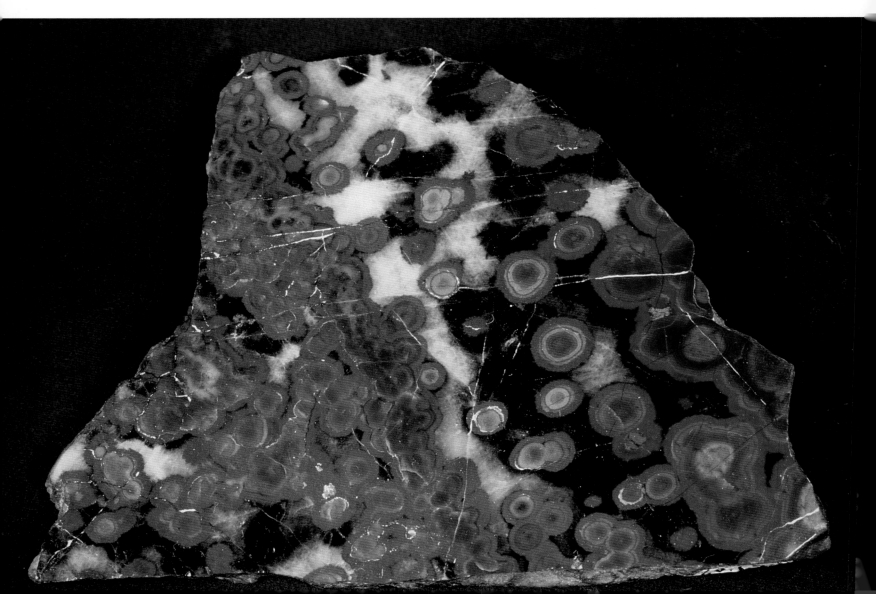

Chrysocolla, like many other copper ores, is a rich blue color and is often cut and polished as an ornamental stone. This specimen clearly exhibits how the copper-rich hydrothermal solution was forced under high heat and pressure into the spaces of another rock.

Twinned staurolite crystals that form at a ninety degree angle are called fairy crosses and are sometimes sold as good luck charms. Staurolite is only formed at great depths in the earth's crust, under extreme temperature and pressure in metamorphic gneiss and schist.

Following page: Gold nuggets often occur with quartz in veins that were formed as metamorphism forced hydrothermal solutions into cracks and crevices in overlying rocks.

refracts the light in the same way water does. Objects appear doubled when viewed through the clear crystals of calcite known as Icelandic spar because of calcite's characteristic double refraction of light.

Some minerals are water soluble and have a distinctive taste: halite tastes salty since it is the same compound as table salt; borax tastes bittersweet; and sylvite tastes bitter. The breathtakingly blue copper mineral chalcanthite is extremely water soluble and tastes both sweet and metallic (but it is poisonous, so this test should be avoided). Smell can also be helpful in identifying a mineral: arsenic minerals generally smell like garlic when heated; many sulfur-containing minerals, such as galena (lead ore), sphalerite (zinc ore), and lazurite smell like rotten eggs when acid is added to them; and bauxite and gibbsite smell like wet clay when breathed upon or moistened.

Some minerals react with the air itself. Nitratine is deliquescent, beading up with water from humid air. Marcasite, a form of iron pyrite which often forms lacy featherlike crystals, becomes brittle and crumbly as it disintegrates into a white powder if left exposed to air on the rock collector's shelf.

The feel of a mineral is also important in identification. Talc is sometimes known as

Iceland spar is a clear crystalline form of calcite, the mineral form of calcium carbonate which also makes up limestone. Iceland spar exhibits double refraction of light—objects viewed through this transparent mineral appear as a double image.

soapstone because it has a soft soapy feel to it. Graphite and molybdenite have a similar slippery texture. Because of this, graphite is often used as a lubricant in machinery. Chrysotile asbestos forms long soft fibers which can be woven into fireproof fabrics; however, it should not be handled because of its ability to cause cancer, especially if microscopic fibers are breathed into the lungs. Mica occurs in thin sheets that can be peeled off into transparent layers that bend and spring back like plastic. Both quartz and obsidian (volcanic glass) feel like glass. Galena, a metallic shiny lead ore with a density that is seven and a half times that of water, has a hefty feel to it.

Every year, thousands of meteorites weighing at least four ounces bombard the earth, but only a few land where they can be retrieved and studied. This is a metallic meteorite composed of nickel and iron. It probably came from the core of an asteroid.

Chrysotile asbestos has a soft fibrous texture. These fibers do not burn, and conduct heat slowly; for this reason they may be woven into fireproof material. However, prolonged exposure to inhaled microscopic particles of asbestos may cause lung cancer.

Garnets come in a variety of colors; grossular garnets such as these can be yellow, brown, pink, green, or colorless. They are formed by contact metamorphism when magma changes shale or mudstone into hornfel.

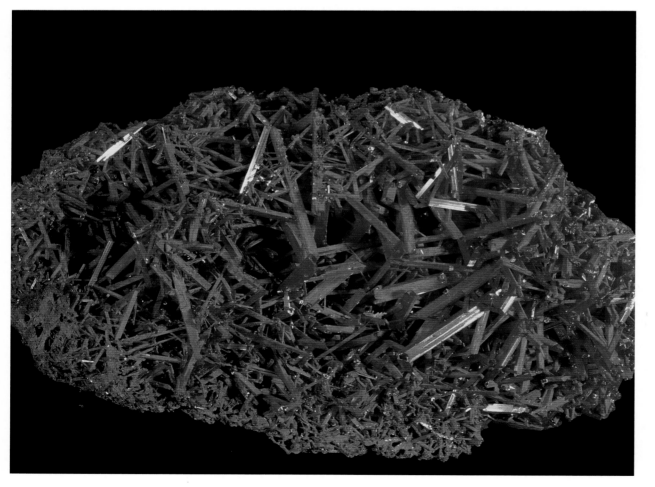

Crocoite is a very rare mineral that contains lead and chromium. It is formed during metamorphism when hot hydrothermal solutions are forced through other rocks, dissolving lead and other minerals that then recrystallize as they cool. This specimen is from Tasmania, Australia.

Petrified wood is usually agate, a type of chalcedony which is a silicate mineral related to quartz. This specimen has perfectly preserved the structure of an extinct relative of the Norfolk Island Pine that lived in Arizona about 200 million years ago: Araucarioxylon arizonicum.

Calcite crystals hang from a limestone cliff along the Rio Grande River in Texas. This calcite formation is called Dogtooth Spar. Both calcite and limestone are made out of calcium carbonate, the same mineral found in chalk, coral, and seashells. Calcium carbonate fizzes when acid is added to it.

Rutilated quartz has fibers of rutile embedded in the crystal. Rutile is a source of titanium, a lightweight, corrosion-resistant metal used in rocket and airplane construction, surgical instruments, bone pins, and paint.

Pyrolusite, an ore of manganese, often forms these lacy, fern-like dendrites which are sometimes mistaken for fossils by beginners. This specimen of pyrolusite dendrite is on a canyon wall in Texas.

The Chemical Composition of Minerals

The chemical composition of minerals determines all of the above properties. Though there are ninety-two naturally occurring elements, only eight of them make up ninety-eight percent (by weight) of the rocks and minerals in the earth's crust. The most common elements are oxygen (forty-seven percent) and silicon (twenty-eight percent), which combine to form the most common group of minerals—the silicates—including such common minerals as quartz, olivine, pyroxene, amphibole, mica, and feldspar. Silicates tend to be hard, transparent or translucent, and of average density.

The next most common element (eight percent) is the most abundant metal in the earth's crust: aluminum. Though it never occurs in nature as pure aluminum, it is found in bauxite (its chief ore), corundum, mica, feldspar, and the clay that is formed from weathered rocks containing these minerals. Iron is the fourth most abundant element found in rocks and minerals, comprising about five percent of the weight of the earth's crust (though it is the most common element in the earth's core). Iron is found in ores, including hematite (its chief ore) and iron pyrite, also known as fool's gold. Both of these are dense, obviously metallic minerals, but iron is also found in many non-metallic

Petrified wood is formed when a hot silica-rich solution permeates the wood. Gradually the wood's organic molecules are replaced by the minerals of the solution, preserving its structure in such intricate detail that we can see the annual growth rings of a twelve million year old Douglas fir tree.

Pyrite has a gold-like luster, but this fool's gold contains no gold. This iron ore is the most common sulfur-containing mineral, and it frequently occurs with sphalerite and galena. Like them, it emits a rotten-egg odor in acid.

minerals, including biotite (black mica), amphiboles, and olivine.

Even though the element calcium is found in less than four percent of the earth's crust, it is a main ingredient in such abundant minerals as dolomite, gypsum, apatite, and calcite. Calcite is the main mineral in limestone and marble. It also comprises the "skeleton" of coral, the shells of mollusks, and the stalactites and stalagmites found in limestone caves. Minerals containing calcium typically fizz and dissolve when acid is added to them.

The remaining elements include three "abundant" ones—sodium, potassium and magnesium—which are each in less than four percent of the earth's crust, and a huge variety of other elements, many of which are rare, extremely useful, and hard to find or extract. An example of one such rare but useful and hard to extract element is germanium. This element is used in television sets and computers, both in the solid state electronics (transistors and diodes) and in the glowing phosphors of the screen. It is also used for infrared night-vision apparatus and for fiber optics. So how is germanium obtained? First the residue left over from zinc refining or from coal ash is heated in the presence of air and chlorine. The chlorine combines with the germanium to make germanium dichloride. When this is mixed with water, the oxygen from water

On the outside, a geode looks like an average rock, but when cut in half it reveals a treasure trove of colorful bands and sparkling crystals.

This black opal from Mexico gets its dazzling play of colors not from the color of the mineral itself, but from the reflection and scattering of light from minuscule spheres of silica within the mineral. Opal forms from silica-rich water that collects in sedimentary rocks or vesicles in volcanic rocks.

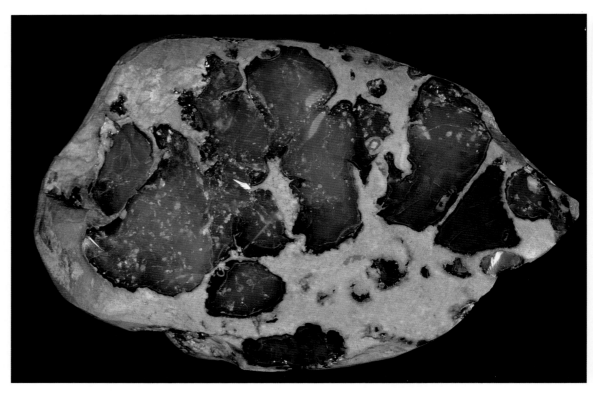

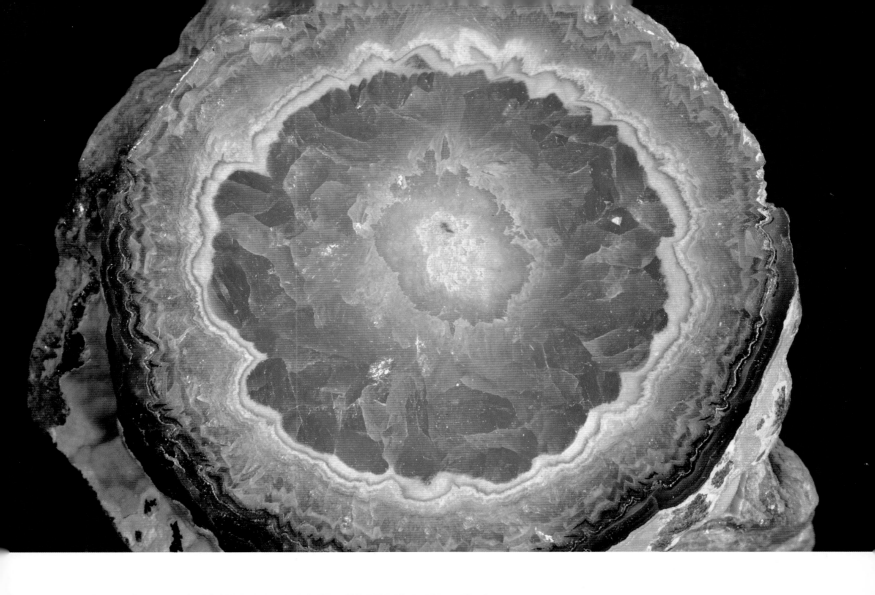

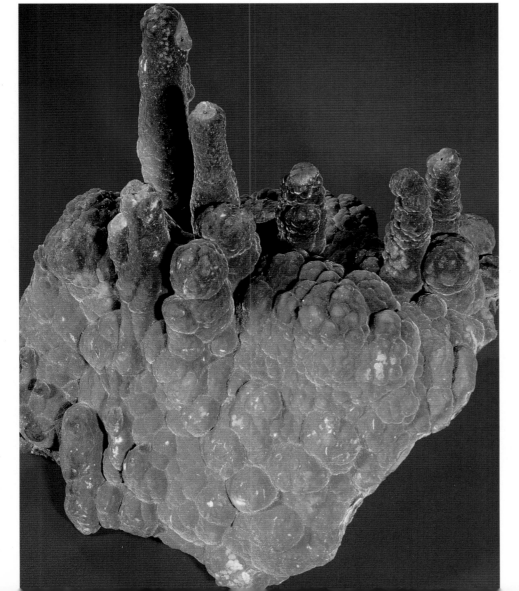

This cross-section of a rhodochrosite stalactite from Argentina was cut and polished to reveal its beautiful pattern of rings. Rhodochrosite is an ore of manganese, a metal which is used to toughen steel alloys for use in machinery, tools, plows, axles and railroad rails.

Malachite, frequently cut and polished as a gemstone, can occur in many forms: botryoidal, incrusting, earthy, or radiating clusters of prismatic crystals. This emerald green group of malachite stalactites was found at a copper mine in Arizona.

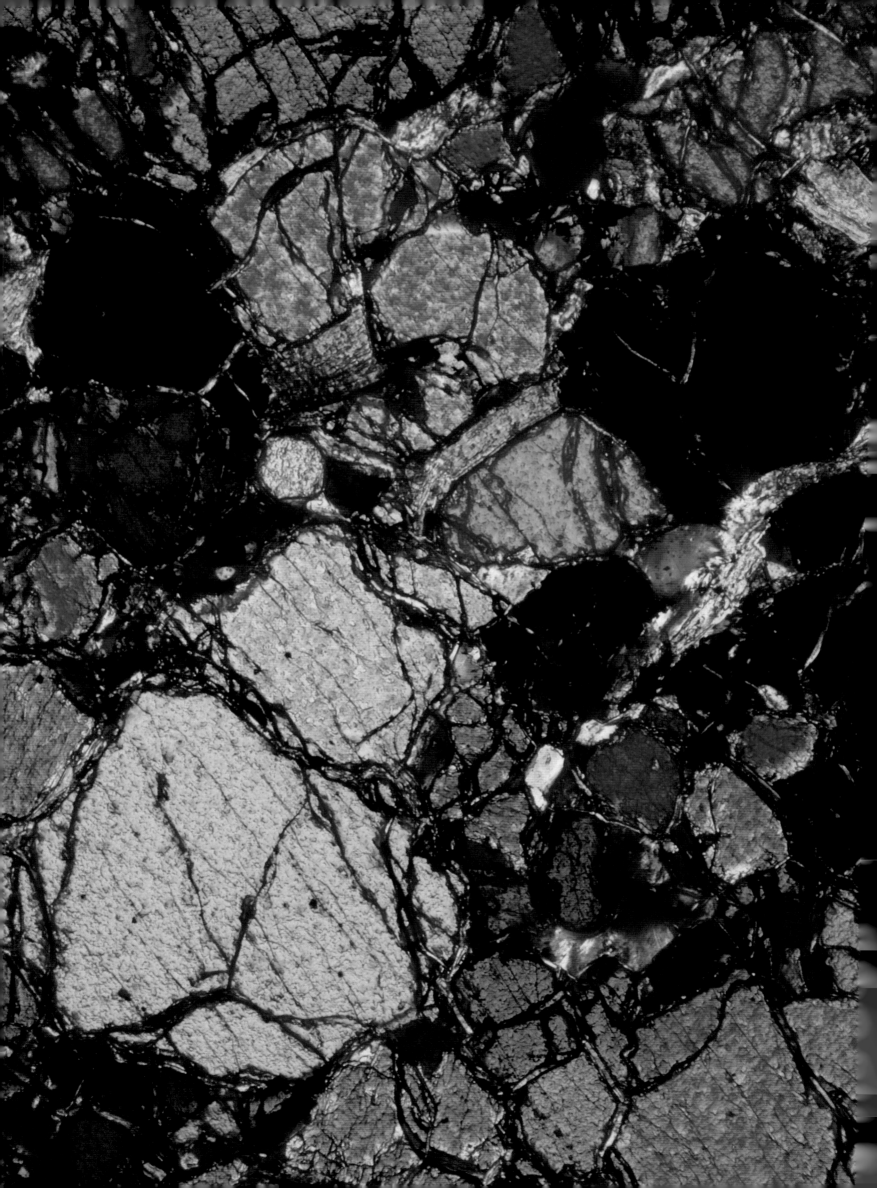

replaces the chlorine resulting in germanium dioxide. Now the oxygen needs to be removed. This is done when hydrogen is added. The hydrogen combines with the oxygen to make water, leaving the germanium metal behind. This germanium is present in extremely small amounts and is still mixed with impurities, so it is purified using a complicated, expensive, and energy-consuming system of repeated melting and recrystallization called zone refining.

Sometimes these less abundant elements are the ones that give the most beauty to a mineral. For instance, quartz is typically a clear crystal but, when tainted by manganese and titanium, it is the pink form called rose quartz; when it contains iron and manganese it is rich purple amethyst; when it contains radium or is exposed to radioactivity, it is dark brown and is known as smoky quartz. Crystals of various minerals may receive their color from chromium in green garnet and red rubies, manganese in pink beryl, magnesium in red garnet, copper in green malachite and blue dioptase, or iron and titanium in blue, yellow, and red sapphires. In the famous Hope Diamond, the rich blue color comes from minute traces of the mineral boron. One atom out every million carbon atoms in this diamond is boron.

Quartz is primarily made out of silica and oxygen, but this amethyst quartz gets its rich violet color from small amounts of iron and manganese incorporated into the silicate matrix.

Impurities of titanium and manganese give rose quartz its watermelon hue.

This microscopic view of a thin slice of peridotite viewed under polarized light reveals the complex mixture of minerals that make up this rock. Peridotite, an intrusive igneous rock, usually contains green olivine and black hornblende. It may also contain colorful flecks of spinel, pyroxene, and garnet.

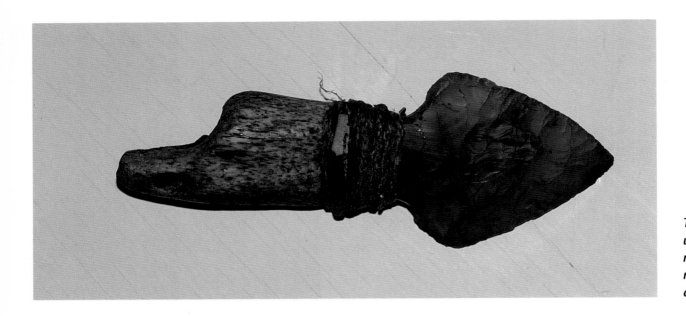

This harpoon head used by Eskimos is made of flint, a silicate mineral related to quartz.

Many minerals can occur in this botry-oidal shape, which resembles a bunch of grapes. This specimen is goethite, an iron ore named after the German poet and philosopher Johann Wolfgang von Goethe, who was also an amateur mineralogist.

Crazy lace agate from Mexico.

ROCKS

What is a Rock?

Rocks are mixtures of distinct minerals in the form of interlocking crystals usually joined by some sort of intergranular cement into a solid structure. Different types of rocks form in different ways under specific conditions, often including intense temperature and pressure. The crystal (grain) size of a rock can indicate how long it took for the rock to cool and solidify, since bigger crystals result from slower cooling. Granite, with its big crystals, cools slower than basalt, with its very fine, barely visible crystals. The types of minerals present in a rock can indicate the temperature and pressure conditions under which that rock was formed, since some minerals, such as olivine and pyroxene, crystallize out of the melted rock solution (magma) at higher temperatures than other minerals, such as quartz.

The three main groups of rocks are the igneous, metamorphic and sedimentary groups. Igneous rocks form from magma as it cools underground near the surface, or when it is expelled during a volcanic eruption. Metamorphic rocks form when the heat of nearby magma causes already-formed rocks to change chemically or to remelt and reform. Sedimentary rocks generally form when erosion deposits weathered rock fragments or dissolved minerals in beds that accumulate to such depth that the resulting pressure compresses the grains, causing them to interlock and become cemented together.

Extrusive Igneous Rocks

What an awesome sight it is to see red-hot globs of magma bursting like fireworks from the top of a volcano or gushing down the slopes as a red, viscous, black-crusted river and then exploding with billowing clouds of

For approximately two billion years, sediments were deposited in an ancient sea in what is now the western United States. Then they were gradually eroded the Colorado River and years of weathering to form the spectacular vistas of the Grand Canyon. Erosion continues today at a rate of about six and a half inches per thousand years.

steam when it hits the ocean. And how frightening it is to hear the thunderous rumblings of a volcano and watch its thick cloud of gray ash slowly and ominously, yet with captivating beauty, climb higher and higher above the cone-shaped peak, drift in the wind, and then silently settle like a smothering snow over everything, burying trees, houses, automobiles, and anything else that couldn't get away in time. One eruption can deposit enough fine particles of ash and cinder to bury a city, such as the famous eruption of Vesuvius, which buried the ancient Roman city of Pompeii in A.D. 79, perfectly preserving its inhabitants and their way of life for us to see today. Flowing lava in Hawaii has been clocked at 58 kilometers per hour gushing out of the volcano at 275 cubic meters per second with temperatures exceeding 2000 degrees Fahrenheit! Most geological processes are so slow and gradual that one is never aware that they are happening. Glaciers grind, sediments settle, continental crusts slide and melt beneath oceanic crusts, mountains uplift as tectonic plates collide undetectably, bit by bit, over millions of years. But the formation of pyroclastic extrusive igneous rocks occurs with such explosive urgency that these rocks are like no others.

Pumice, belched into the air from a volcano, cools so quickly that it traps bubbles of gas and air in its porous, glasslike structure. As a result, it is the only rock that floats, often drifting for thousands of miles in oceanic currents before washing up on some distant shore.

Sometimes a fine spray of erupting magma will quickly cool into long greenish brown strands of glass that look like clumps of hair. This is called "Pelee's hair."

Obsidian, a sleek, black volcanic glass, forms when silica-rich lava cools so quickly that there is no time for crystals to form. Prehistoric people highly valued this rock because it was easily cleaved and sculpted into hunting and cutting tools with very sharp edges. A chunk of this rock looks shiny black, but very thin slices are transparent.

Pumice and obsidian are forms of rhyolite. Rhyolitic magma has the same chemical composition as granite and is more viscous than basaltic or andesitic lavas, which also form from volcanoes. As a result, rhyolitic lavas tend to cool and form a plug in the

Granite is an intrusive igneous rock which forms from magma deep in the earth's crust. Its relatively large crystals indicate that it cools slowly. In this photo the minerals quartz (glassy gray), potassium feldspar (pink), and hornblende (black) can be seen.

As the flowing surface of basaltic lava cools, its viscous skin wrinkles into ropy patterns of pahoehoe lava, or folds into jagged chunks of aa lava. Sometimes a thick-walled lava tube is formed. In this photo, molten lava can be seen flowing through the lava tube.

Obsidian, also known as volcanic glass, is formed when silica-rich lava cools so quickly that there is no time for crystals to form. Because it can be easily chipped to form edges as sharp as glass, it was frequently used by prehistoric man to make knives, spearpoints, and hand-axes.

middle of the crater blocking the magma flow until pressure builds up and explodes violently, blasting away the top of the mountain. Sometimes airborne globs of lava will cool and harden into twisted spindle shapes perhaps a meter long—volcanic "bombs" that may leave small impact craters when they land!

Eruptions also produce massive amounts of finely grained ash that can stay suspended in the air and carried by wind currents for weeks, resulting in beautiful sunsets all over the world. The Mount Pinatubo eruption in the Philippines in 1991 produced some spectacular sunsets in the eastern United States. As successive eruptions eject more and more ash and more coarsely grained cinders, these particles settle together and become interlocked, due to the weight of the deposits above, producing a rock called tuff. Often tuff deposits are stratified, each layer representing a different eruption. These deposits erode fairly quickly compared to the more solid rhyolitic plug that may have filled the crater. This plug may remain standing long after all the tuff has eroded away. Some famous geological landmarks such as Le Puy de Dôme in France were formed in this way.

Basalt is the most common extrusive igneous rock. It is found in massive lava flows that cover thousands of square miles, sometimes accumulating to depths of thousands of feet. For example, the Hawaiian islands are the result of repeated basaltic lava flows. Mauna Kea is the tallest mountain in Hawaii. If one takes into consideration that Mauna Kea's base is over 19,000 feet deep at the

Basalt columns, such as these at Latourell Falls in Oregon's Columbia River Gorge, may be formed when rapid cooling causes the basalt to fracture into hexagonal columns. The yellow in this photo is lichen growing on the rocks. The trail provides an idea of the size of these columns.

Anasazi took advantage of the friable nature of tuff by carving their apartment-style cliff dwellings into these tuff cliffs at Bandelier National Monument in New Mexico. Tuff is made from volcanic ash.

Red-hot basaltic lava spews out of the depths of the Hawaii's Kilauea volcano producing ash, volcanic bombs, and red rivers of lava which cool on top forming a black crust or viscous skin.

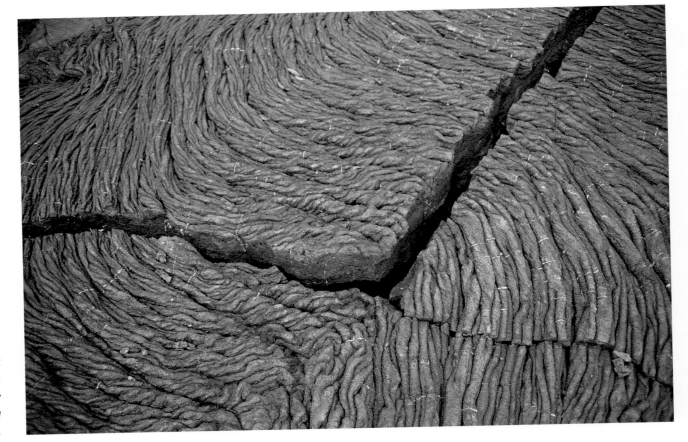

Pahoehoe lava forms when the surface of flowing lava cools into a viscous slow-moving goo that wrinkles into this rope-like texture before hardening into a crust.

The view from inside a lava tube formed in the Galapagos Islands of Ecuador. This lava tube is over a kilometer long and is wide enough for several people to walk through side-by-side.

These sea lions are sunning themselves on a tuff formation in the Galapagos Islands. Tuff is formed by deposits of volcanic ash—this formation clearly shows the stratification formed by successive eruptions.

When basalt cools, its bubbling surface is often pocked with nooks and crannies. Later these vesicles can be filled with crystalline deposits such as the calcite in this specimen of amygdaloidal basalt.

bottom of the ocean and its peak is 13,796 feet above sea level, it could be considered the tallest mountain in the world.

As basaltic lava flows, the top cools like the skim on the top of a cup of good homemade cocoa. As the fluid rock flows, the top crust flows along with it, usually in one of two typical patterns. Runnier lava flows smoothly, its crust wrinkling into wonderful patterns of ropy pahoehoe lava. The more viscous lava hardens into thicker crusts as it flows. This crust breaks into pieces that roll over into sharp, jagged fragments. These fragments, called *aa*, can still tear a hiker's sneakers to pieces decades later. Sometimes the lava surface hardens into a tube with molten lava flowing through it. When the eruption stops, the lava flows out of the tube, leaving a hollow tunnel, perhaps several kilometers long, that is tall and wide enough for several people to hike through side by side.

Basaltic lava that is at the surface often hardens full of gas pockets, looking like a severely burned English muffin. This vesicular form of basalt is called *scoria*. Later, when this basalt is buried under more deposits, these nooks and crannies can become filled with beautiful deposits of copper, agate, calcite, or one of a group of minerals called zeolites, which form delicate clumps of radiating crystals. This mineral-filled scoria is called *amygdaloidal* basalt.

Another event associated with volcanoes is the venting of volcanic gases rich in minerals, especially sulfur; hence the rotten egg smell and the stinging eyes from sulfur dioxide when one stands downwind of these fumaroles. The rocks around these fumaroles are frequently caked with a crust of yellow sulfur deposits. Cinnabar (mercury ore) and stibnite (antimony ore) can also be found here.

Intrusive Igneous Rocks

When magma crystallizes and solidifies before it reaches the surface of the earth, it forms intrusive igneous rocks. Intrusive igneous rocks are also called *plutonic* rocks, named after Pluto, the Greek god of the Underworld. Plutonic magma, forced by pressures from below, may intrude between rock layers or into cracks in rocks, forming horizontal sills and vertical or angled dikes of granite or pegmatite. Or it may push up the surface rock layers from below, forming a dome of mountains above it. This type of igneous formation is called a *batholith* and is usually granite. Batholiths may form several kilometers below the ground and may be several hundred kilometers long, forming the roots of an entire mountain range . Typically, intrusive magma cools more slowly than extrusive magma so the structure of these rocks—unlike the finely grained texture of basalt and rhyolite or the glasslike, noncrystalline texture of obsidian—consists of coarse, easily distinguished crystals.

The best known intrusive igneous rock is granite. It has large, easily identified crystals about five millimeters long. Granite is one of the last rocks to form as magma cools, so its crystals are from minerals that form at lower temperatures after other minerals have crystallized out in the process of forming other

igneous rocks such as gabbro and peridotite. The pale pink and creamy white grains in granite are feldspar. Feldspar makes up about sixty percent of a typical granite. The gray grains which comprise about thirty percent of a granite are quartz. Shiny silvery or black flecks are mica. Black hard grains are hornblende. Sometimes the granite is red due to the presence of iron in the form of hematite flakes. Graphic granite has an interesting pattern of zigzagging gray quartz crystals that

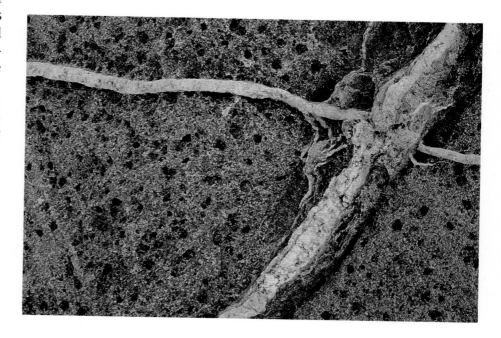

When plutonic magma intrudes into faults and fractures in bedrock and then cools, it forms horizontal sills and vertical or angled dikes of a different mineral composition from the surrounding rock.

Cinnabar is the most common ore of mercury. Since mercury has a low boiling point, it is often deposited around hot springs and steam vents when the temperature drops to a point where the mercury can condense. Liquid mercury is so dense that iron can float in it.

look like writing embedded in a creamy feldspar background. This pattern forms when the quartz and feldspar crystallize simultaneously.

One of the first intrusive igneous rocks to form from cooling magma is gabbro. Its large grains indicate that it cools slowly, as granite does, but it is a much darker rock since it has no quartz and has several dark minerals such as olivine, pyroxene, and augite. These dark minerals crystallize at higher temperatures than the minerals that form granite. Often the deeper layers of gabbro are rich in iron (hematite or magnetite), chromium (chromite), or nickel (nickeline); because these crystallize at high temperatures and are more dense, they settle to the bottom of the magma chamber before it solidifies. These minerals commonly form large ore deposits that are mined extensively.

Pegmatite has the same chemical composition as granite but it contains an amazing abundance of large, well-formed crystals. It is not unusual to find crystals several inches long. In fact spodumene crystals over fifty feet long and weighing eighty tons have been found in pegmatites in the Black Hills of South Dakota. Pegmatite deposits are excellent places to look for such rare or beautiful gem minerals as beryl, tourmaline, opal, topaz, and zircon. Industrial minerals are also mined from pegmatites: corundum for

One of the most prized gems is emerald, the green form of beryl, a mineral which often occurs in pegmatite and some metamorphic rocks. The most valuable emeralds have a velvety appearance with an even distribution of color. Emerald is harder than quartz but is not as hard as ruby or sapphire.

Sapphire is a gem form of the mineral corundum. It can come in a variety of colors including blue, pink, yellow, green, violet, and even orange.

Stromatolites are some of the oldest fossils known— over a billion years old. Australian Cyanobacteria still grow today in cabbage-like clumps resembling these fossilized ones from the Rocky Mountains of Montana. These bacteria form limestone by secreting protective layers of calcium carbonate.

As magma cooled slowly at great depth, relatively large block-like crystals of feldspar began to form in the molten mass. Then the magma quickly moved toward the surface forming a matrix of smaller-grained crystals as it cooled more rapidly. Such rocks are called porphyries.

51

polishing and abrasive uses; spodumene and lepidolite for the metal lithium, which is used for pacemaker batteries, rocket propellants, a variety of pharmaceuticals, and the synthesis of vitamin A; and "rare earth" minerals such as yttrium, used for lasers and color television screens, lanthanum, used for lighter flints and catalytic converters, and thulium, used as a source of x-rays. Metal ores are also often associated with pegmatites: cassiterite for tin, manganite for manganese, and hematite for iron.

How is pegmatite formed? As magma cools, more and more minerals crystallize out, leaving a watery and gaseous solution of minerals above the crystallized magma. Eventually this all crystallizes into a pegmatite body in whatever shape the surrounding rocks allow. It can be lens-shaped, table-like, pipe-like, or irregularly-branched and it can exceed several kilometers in length, though most pegmatite deposits are much smaller: 30 to 300 meters long and 1 to 30 meters wide.

Porphyries are igneous rocks that are identified by their varying crystal sizes rather than by their mineral composition. Porphyries can be extrusive or intrusive igneous rocks, but they are all formed in basically the same way. As the magma cools slowly at a great depth, relatively large block-like crystals (phenocrysts) of feldspar, quartz,

Tufa deposits exposed by low water levels at Pyramid Lake in Nevada. Tufa is formed when calcium carbonate precipitates out of lime-rich water as the water evaporates and the mineral concentration increases. Sometimes plants and animals can be preserved in tufa, which can cover them in just a few months.

Our best insect fossils occur in the mineral amber— plant sap which was fossilized after trapping insects in its sticky goo, protecting them from decay and preserving the intricate details of their structure. These ants from twenty-four to fifty-four million years ago are very similar to modern ants.

or biotite (black mica) form. But then something suddenly forces the magma to the surface, where the rest of the minerals crystallize quickly into a more finely grained matrix surrounding the phenocrysts. Breccia and conglomerate are other rocks that have large chunky pieces embedded in a finer matrix. But they are both sedimentary rocks that can be easily distinguished from porphyry by looking at the shape of the rock chunks. Conglomerate has rounded pebbles, eroded by water as they were carried long distances before being deposited in the mud or sand they were preserved in. Breccia has angular fragments of a variety of sizes and shapes because it is made up of resolidified fragments that were blasted out of crater walls by volcanic eruptions, or chipped off cliffs by the expansion of freezing ice in rock cracks, or sheered off along fault lines by earthquakes as the two sides of the fault were thrust past each other.

Hydrothermal Veins

Water is a volatile component of magma. It boils upward as superheated steam under great pressure. As it rises through the crust it dissolves minerals out of the rocks and becomes increasingly mineral-laden. As it rises, its pressure and temperature drop and it is exposed to cool groundwater percolating down through the rock from the surface, which may be as much as a mile above. These conditions cause the less soluble minerals to precipitate out as crystals in fissures, cavities, and tiny pores in the rock. The crystals deposited in cracks are called veins; those in cavities are called vugs. Veins may range from a few millimeters to tens of meters wide and may be several kilometers long. Although the most common mineral component in veins and vugs is quartz, these deposits are often mined for their concentrations of gold, silver, metal ores, gemstones, and other minerals of industrial importance, especially where

When hot hydrothermal solutions of minerals bubble out of the ground in geysers and hot springs, the rapid cooling forms deposits of minerals. Mammoth Hot Springs in Yellowstone National Park is surrounded by a square mile of travertine dissolved from limestone bedrock and redeposited at a rate of two tons per day.

mountain building and erosion have exposed them at the earth's surface. Each of these minerals is deposited in a sequence determined by their relative solubility under specific conditions of temperature and pressure. Iron and sphalerite (zinc) deposits occur in the hottest areas, and cinnabar (mercury), sulfur, and stibnite (antimony) occur in the coolest areas, including where the boiling mineral broth reaches the surface as hot mineral springs.

Sedimentary Rocks

When rocks are exposed at the surface, even the hardest of them erodes away, grain by grain, over millions of years. The Appalachians of the eastern United States were probably the size of the present-day Himalayas about 250 million years ago. Now their highest peaks seem like hills compared to the Himalayas or the Rockies.

Throughout the millennia, rain, with its slightly acidic pH, dissolved carbonates and other minerals out of the rocks. So did plant life—lichens—which secrete an acid to etch a foothold for themselves into the rocks. Wind, rain, and ice worked their way into the little crevices. Depressions formed by this chemical weathering lifted out the tougher minerals like quartz, making sand. Since water expands when it freezes, each winter, with its almost daily cycles of freezing and thawing, caused significant erosion.

Clay, composed of very fine grained particles of aluminum-rich minerals such as feldspar and mica, was formed from the weathering of rocks such as granite, phyllite, and schist. These particles of clay and sand eventually were carried by rain and melt water into mountain streams and then into rivers like the Shenandoah and the Potomac. They were used by these rushing rivers as abrasives, grinding away at any exposed rock until eventually the grains were deposited in the sea as sediments.

On a visit to the clay and sandstone cliffs that border Chesapeake Bay, one can see layer

Following page: The corrugated texture of these sandstone pinnacles is due to differential erosion rates since different sediments have different hardnesses. Extensive talus slopes accumulate at the foot of mountains as ice, rain, and wind erode chunks of rock from the cliffs.

Quartz sand grains are relatively resistant to erosion, unlike most other minerals which easily degrade into finer-grained clay or dissolve in solution, leaving the quartz grains to be carried away and deposited by wind and rain. Red sandstone gets its rusty color iron oxide.

This wonderfully-sculptured slot canyon in Arizona was probably created as a stream etched its way through relatively resistant sandstone in an arid region where very little weathering occurs. Weathering widens canyons after a river makes the initial incision.

upon layer of these particles from the Appalachians, deposited about ten to twenty million years ago in a shallow sea that is now dry land. The sharks, rays, whales, manatees, crocodiles, coral, and shellfishes that once inhabited this sea were buried in these sediments. As the Appalachians shrank from the forces of erosion, the sediments deepened, and the whole mass of sand, clay, and animal remains was transformed into sedimentary rock, compacted by the weight of hundreds of feet of overlying sediments and cemented together by the minerals dissolved in the intergranular fluids. The bones, teeth, and

shells of these extinct organisms can be seen in layers in the cliffs and can be found along many of the beaches of Chesapeake Bay. The same process has occurred countless times all over the world. In fact, it has even occurred at least once before in the region of the Appalachians. Some of the rock that was uplifted to form the towering Appalachians was full of fossilized trilobites that were buried beneath sediments in an even more ancient sea 375 million years ago. These fossils can still be found today in road cuts through some of the oldest rocks near the bases of the mountains.

These harbor seals in Oregon have hauled themselves out to bask in the sun on a sandstone formation that clearly shows a variety of sedimentary strata and cross-bedding.

Fossil deposits of clams (Isocardia) form bands in the clay cliffs that border the Chesapeake Bay and its tributary rivers such as the Mattaponi River in Virginia. They were deposited around fifteen million years ago under an ancient sea.

An undersea drama has been frozen in time, preserved in sandstone in the Green River formation of Wyoming for all to see. A Diplomystus *fish* was eating a Priscacara *fish* about fourty-five million years ago, when an unknown catastrophe killed it and buried them both in sediment.

Trilobites, such as these Homotelus bromidensis *preserved in some Oklahoma mud about 435–500 million years ago, are now extinct. All that we know about them has been learned from evidence preserved in rocks.*

As sediment settles in bodies of water it preserves plants, animals, or signs of animals as fossils. Here, preserved in sandstone, is a fossil track of an unknown animal that roamed the sand flats 500 million years ago. This mystery animal has been named Climactichnites.

So, one category of sedimentary rock, often rich in fossils, is formed from deposits of sand or clay, compacted to perhaps fifty percent of its original volume, and glued together with some sort of intergranular cement such as silica, iron oxide, or calcite. These are the sandstones, mudstones, and shales. Some limestones are also formed in this way, especially those that are rich in fossil shells or coral.

Some limestones, however, are formed in a more chemical way, especially in tropical, warm-water environments. Dissolved calcium carbonate (calcite), derived from the chemical erosion of terrestrial rock or from seashells, coral, algae, or microscopic organisms, can build up in layers around a bit of seashell or a sand grain to form beads that settle and become oolitic limestone. Calcium carbonate solution can also permeate clay sediments and form marl limestone. Spectacular "artwork" often forms in caves and crevices where water seeps down through limestone, dissolving and redepositing the calcite: stalactites, stalagmites, travertine "waterfalls," lacy branches of aragonite and crystals of the aptly named dogtooth spar.

Other sedimentary rocks, chalk for instance, are made from sediment derived purely from the remains of organisms. Chalk is formed from deposits of calcite-shelled microscopic organisms related to the amoeba that have settled to the bottom of the ocean over the millennia. Opal, chert, and flint can be formed from similar deposits of organisms, such as sea sponges or microscopic diatoms, which have silica (a glasslike mineral) in their shells instead of calcite.

Fossil fuels—petroleum, natural gas, and coal—are also formed from the remains of prehistoric organisms. Because of this and because of their inconsistent and organic molecule content, they generally are not considered true minerals. Petroleum and natural gas first formed when microscopic plankton settled into the sand and mud of calm, shallow bays ten to twenty million years ago and were probably converted to their present forms (organic hydrocarbons) under high pressure anaerobic conditions between 100 and 200 degrees Celsius. When these deposits were later uplifted and folded, these hydrocarbons were forced up through the pores in the rock by water or pressure and accumulated in faults or in pockets beneath a less permeable arched rock layer at the top of a fold.

This red mudstone from several thousand feet elevation in the Rockies of Glacier National Park, Montana, tells us that once there was a calm lowland body of water here that dried up forming, these preserved mud cracks which were later covered with a lighter-colored sediment.

The Continental Divide at Gunsight Pass in Glacier National Park shows layers of red mudstones, bent and folded as they were uplifted from flat, muddy lowlands to towering mountain peaks by tremendous, but slow-acting, geological forces.

Coal is formed mostly from plants that lived between 270 and 350 million years ago. These plants were buried in swamps in anaerobic conditions, similar to those in Georgia's Okefenokee Swamp, that prevented their decomposition. The sea level rose and sediments of sand and mud were piled on top of the swamps. The resulting high pressure and temperature drove out the water and many of the volatile chemicals in the plants, leaving behind a carbon-rich coal. Over the millennia this cycle of alternating swamp and sea has repeated itself several times, forming layers of sandstone, shale, and coal. The higher the pressure and temperature, the higher the coal's carbon percentage becomes. Bituminous coal is the most common type, but it is softer and dirtier than anthracite coal, which produces much less of the pollutant sulfur dioxide when it is burned. During the industrial revolution the beautiful intricate details of sculptures and statues in Europe began to erode into faceless masses. The sulfur dioxide produced by the burning of coal and oil mixed with the water in the air to make acid, which dissolves calcite-based minerals such as the limestone out of which these statues were carved.

The last category of sedimentary rocks are the evaporites. These form where evaporation of mineral-rich water leaves behind a crusty deposit of minerals. The great expanses of evaporite salt flats show the location of extinct inland seas. Some halite (rock salt) deposits may be as much as four hundred meters deep. They may cover hundreds of thousands of square kilometers. Such huge accumulations were probably formed by the repeated refilling and re-evaporation of these inland seas. Other evaporites are apatite, borax, dolomite, epsomite and gypsum, all of which have a multitude of industrial uses.

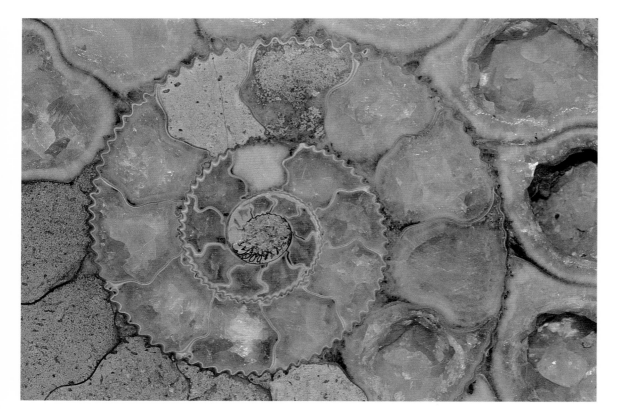

This fossilized ammonite (Parkinsonia dorsetensis) from 174–164 million years ago shows calcite crystals derived from limestone in some of its originally-hollow chambers.

This beautiful abstract sculpture was etched by rainwater on the top of limestone cliffs along the Rio Grande in Mexico. The rain dissolves the calcium carbonate, which may eventually crystallize as calcite or be used by coral and clams to make their shells hundreds of miles away in the Gulf of Mexico.

Of all the metamorphic rocks, gneiss is formed under the highest temperature and pressure conditions and displays the highest degree of metamorphic change. The crystals are generally larger and more easily identified than in schist, as exemplified in this specimen of hornblende gneiss.

This biotite gneiss exhibits a third pattern in which gneiss can occur. Biotite is black mica. Banding in metamorphic rocks is aligned perpendicular to the direction of pressure.

Metamorphic Rocks

Metamorphosis is the Greek word for transformation. Metamorphic rocks are rocks that have been transformed by the intense temperature of intruding magma, or the massive pressure associated with mountain formation, or a high temperature gas or mineral solution forced through their pores. During metamorphism, while the rocks are still solid or slightly plastic, the mineral grains are rearranged into bands or layers. Crystals may grow, and the chemistry of minerals may change. Changed by the heat of the intruding magma, metamorphic rocks form fifty-meter-wide aureoles around small igneous batholiths, narrow metamorphic zones along igneous dikes and sills, and huge masses covering hundreds of square kilometers around the cores of mountains. The type and characteristics of a metamorphic rock depends primarily on the temperature and pressure conditions under which it was formed and the type of rock it was formed from. At about 150 degrees Celsius and about 10 kilometers below the surface, the minerals of shale are forced to line up in layers perpendicular to the force exerted on them. This changes some forms of shale into slate. Slate is easily split along these lines, which is why it is so easily made into flagstones, roofing tiles, and blackboards. Low temperature and low pressure metamorphism will convert other forms of shale to phyllite, whose fine grains of sparkling mica give it a silky luster.

Greenstone is igneous basalt that has been metamorphosed into a compact, unbanded slaty rock that is rich in the green minerals chlorite and epidote. Often narrow veins of quartz or calcite traverse it, as in this 600 million-year-old specimen in the Blue Ridge Mountains of Virginia.

Sandstone is changed to quartzite by metamorphism. Often the banding produced by sedimentation is still visible as in these quartzite boulders. Since sandstone breaks along the intergranular cement it generally feels gritty, while quartzite, which breaks through the grains, feels smoother.

This close-up view of mica schist shows the finer crystal size and less distinct banding of schist. The silvery flecks are muscovite mica; the black flecks are biotite mica. Mica schist may also contain small amounts of quartz, feldspar, garnet, and greenish chlorite.

Sometimes phyllite has a greenish hue from chlorite.

In areas where medium to high temperature and pressure has been applied, shale is converted to schist. There are many kinds of schists, classified by their most conspicuous minerals. Garnet-mica schist may have large wine-colored garnets embedded in a silvery sparkling matrix of black or greenish mica. Garnets form best where temperatures are 250 to 450 degrees Celsius. Kyanite-staurolite schist will form at even higher temperatures (up to 700 degrees Celsius) 6 to 9 miles below the surface near the center of a mountain belt. Kyanite often forms beautiful sky blue crystals perpendicular to the metamorphic force. Staurolite sometimes forms a black, cross-shaped crystal known as a "fairy cross," which is sometimes sold as a lucky charm.

Eclogite and gneiss are formed under the highest temperature and pressure metamorphism. Gneiss is probably a major ingredient of the lower continental crust. It is usually banded and, like schist, it is identified primarily by its most conspicuous minerals and the type of rock from which it was formed. It can be distinguished from schist by its generally more distinct banding (formed when pressure caused minerals to crystallize together into parallel bands) and by its lack of "schistosity," which refers to the wavy, irregular edges that schist forms when it breaks.

When limestone and dolomite are metamorphosed, they become marble. The greater the temperature and pressure during metamorphism, the larger the crystals. Often marble is swirled with beautiful patterns due to impurities. When igneous rocks are metamorphosed, they become gneiss, amphibolite, and serpentinite. Sandstone is metamorphosed to quartzite. Bituminous coal is metamorphosed by pressure to anthracite (increasing its carbon content), and by high temperature intrusions to graphite. Graphite and diamond are both one hundred percent carbon, but they are on opposite extremes of the hardness scale. Why? It has to do with how the atoms of carbon are arranged. In graphite each carbon is attached to three others, primarily on one plane, forming sheets of carbon which easily slide past each other, hence its excellent use as a lubricant. In diamond each carbon is attached to four

carbons, including above and below, forming a solid immovable crystalline structure.

Besides changing by temperature and pressure, metamorphic rocks can be changed by the injection of hot aqueous mineral solutions and gases arising from igneous intrusions. As these hot mineral solutions permeate through the rock, some minerals are replaced by others, new crystals grow, and the rock chemistry changes. These are generally called hydrothermal replacement deposits, and they are usually excellent places to find ores of copper, tin, zinc, lead and iron as well as gems like garnet, topaz, tourmaline and sapphire. This is also the way spectacular pieces of petrified wood are formed. A hot silica solution removes the wood molecules one by one and replaces them with silica, perfectly preserving the wood's grain, growth rings, and insect burrows!

When limestone undergoes metamorphism it is changed to marble. This unpolished marble also contains swirls of green serpentine and would make an extremely attractive ornamental block if cut and polished.

Afterword

Where would we be without rocks and minerals? They affect us in every way imaginable. They provide the raw materials for almost every object we use. They provide energy to power almost everything we do. They determine soil type and local ecology. They help farmers grow the foods we eat. They tell us about the history of the earth. And they dazzle our eyes and inspire our hearts with their spectacular beauty.

But as we gather and process these minerals, we usually damage the environment. In the United States, an area the size of Connecticut has been excavated to obtain minerals. Toxic leachates and by-products of smelting and refining pollute our environment. There is a finite supply of all minerals, and most of them are getting harder to find and more difficult to extract. Petroleum is so important to the chemical and plastics industries that many people wonder about the wisdom of burning it as a fuel. Many countries have regulations and industries designed to encourage recycling, limit pollution, and restore mine sites to healthy ecosystems. Still, there is a tremendous waste of resources and considerable pollution as we bury or incinerate our trash.

Please do all you can to reduce, reuse, and recycle in order to conserve our precious mineral resources.

Coal is formed by deposits of plants that are buried beneath sediments in swamps where they cannot decompose quickly. Coal beds are a great place to find plant fossils such as these 300 million-year-old seed ferns (Alethopteris).

This sample of banded or folded gneiss shows that the banding pattern is often more distinct in gneiss than in schist.

INDEX

*Page numbers in **bold-face** type indicate photo captions.*